MR. FLIPPY'S
LAND FLIPPING HANDBOOK

MR. FLIPPY'S
LAND FLIPPING HANDBOOK
"WEALTH & RICHES WITH DIRT & DITCHES"

WILLIAM VAUGHN IV

PALMETTO
PUBLISHING
Charleston, SC
www.PalmettoPublishing.com

Mr. Flippy's Land Flipping Handbook
Copyright © 2024 by William Vaughn IV

All rights reserved

No portion of this book may be reproduced, stored in a retrieval system, or transmitted in any form by any means–electronic, mechanical, photocopy, recording, or other–except for brief quotations in printed reviews, without prior permission of the author.

First Edition

Paperback ISBN: 979-8-8229-5469-4
eBook ISBN: 979-8-8229-5470-0

Table Of Contents

Chapter 1
The Secret Niche Of Land Flipping 1

Chapter 2
The Simplicity of Land Flipping. 10

Chapter 3
Land Flipping Success Habits. 22

Confessions of a
WINNER & OVERCOMER

(Say These Power Statements Below Out Loud Before You Read This Book!)

---

* Right now, I commit to be a WINNER & OVERCOMER in every area of my life.

* I no longer settle for a life of mediocrity and defeat.

* I am determined and 100% willing to change whatever I need to change in me and around me to live a TRIUMPHANT life.

* My HUNGER to WIN is GREATER than every obstacle I face.

* I only allow thoughts of VICTORY, SUCCESS, and WINNING POSSIBILITIES to remain in my mind.

* I only permit relationships in my inner circle that EMPOWER my WINNING LIFESTYLE.

* I immediately and unapologetically separate from anything and anyone that attempts to hold me back from GOD-GIVEN DESTINY.

* I boldly declare that my days of losing and my days of LIMITATIONS ARE OVER.

* From this moment forward I choose to THINK LIKE A WINNER, TALK LIKE A WINNER, and LIVE LIKE A WINNER, because through GOD'S POWER I am a WINNER & OVERCOMER.

(If you just said those words out loud and really believe it, then you are on your way to extracting the content of this book to see life-changing results in your financial and personal life.)

CHAPTER 1

"THE SECRET NICHE OF LAND FLIPPING"

How It All Began

I was sitting at my office desk and this thought consumed my mind. "*If I don't do something different today, I will wake up 10 years from now and be in the same exact position.*" I remember that thought like it was yesterday. I was about to be 29 years old and I had the sudden realization that the trajectory of my life and financial status was not what I wanted it to be. I knew I had to do something different if I wanted to get different results in my life.

That's when my pursuit of real estate investing really began. I always had an interest in real estate but I was busy pursuing other ventures and responsibilities in life so it wasn't a top priority up to that point. But when I realized I wasn't getting any younger and that time wasn't waiting on me, I had to get moving towards my true potential.

I started soaking up all the knowledge I could find on how to get started in real estate and the quickest way to start making actual money. I read books, I listened to videos, I attended meetings – whatever it took to start getting different results in my life I was willing to do it.

On my journey of acquiring knowledge, I came to the proverbial "fork in the road." I had been seeking out all the free knowledge I could. Then I was faced with an opportunity to start getting mentorship, but it came at a price tag. I didn't have a lot of money at that time but I had a lot of hunger and desire to get results so I was going to find a way to make it work. The real estate mentorship cost $5,000. I had a little money saved up but not enough for the whole course. "Coincidentally" soon after this course came available, my wife and I were offered a free trip from a family member to go on a cruise. They were going to pay for it 100% for us. That was a no brainer! We had never been on a cruise before and wanted to go, but my hunger to see better results in my life was greater than my desire to go on a cruise at that moment. I negotiated with my family member and asked them instead of buying the tickets for the cruise would they let me use that same money to buy this real estate course. They were skeptical and thought it was just a scam or "get rich quick scheme." I knew deep down inside that I could make real money in real estate with the right guidance and help and that some way some how I was going to be rich one day in the real estate business. They finally agreed to let me use the money for the course instead of the cruise. My thought was with the knowledge and skills I was about to get I could pay for my own cruise or even my cruise ship one day if I wanted. I was off to the races now!

Once I began the mentorship course, I was at the point of no return. I did everything I could think of to get that elusive 1st deal. I cold called. I mailed post cards. I sent text messages. I knocked on doors. I put out signs in the yard. Week after week and month after month passed and still no deal. But I wasn't quitting until I finally got it. Then after about 6 months it finally happened. I got my 1st deal! It was a wholesale deal on a single family house where I simply "assigned" my contract with the seller to an investor who wanted to fix up the house. I made a whopping $1,775.00! But that isn't the whole story. I ended up getting someone to help me find that buyer so I had to 50/50 split the $1,775.00 leaving me with a grand total of $887.50. Now I know what you're thinking reading this book. You're probably like *"You worked hard for 6 months to only make $887.50 on a deal?"* Even though the "amount" wasn't that high the "experience" was worth everything. I knew the process actually worked. Now all I had to do was find some more deals with a few more 0's.

Once I had that confidence boost of closing my first deal, I got the momentum I needed to start doing more deals. I wholesaled several more houses. I completed a couple of flips where I had the property renovated and resold it. I even acquired a couple of rentals using creative financing strategies such as owner financing and subject-to. I was on my way to being rich! *Or was I?*

I was finally starting to see some results in my business and had the proof that it really did work, but I was lacking one key ingredient of lasting success – *healthy business relationships*. Even though I was starting to make money in real estate I still had certain people around me who either had ulterior motives or who gave me bad counsel on projects so I had to learn several lessons the good ole' fashioned hard way. Losing money! I jokingly tell people if there are 1,000 ways to lose your money, I have discovered 999 of them (I'm still looking for that last one – lol). From $55,000 being stolen on a project, to being scammed out of another $100,000, to not having a good agent on a deal causing me to have to pay $20,000 out of pocket at closing on a deal, I had my fair share of disappointments and setbacks. Experiencing these financial hurdles and difficulties caused me to not be able to meet certain obligations and commitments threatening my reputation and relationships with people that were close to me. I was at a real crossroad in my life. My dream of getting rich in real estate appeared to be becoming a nightmare.

The Missing Piece To My Success

As all of these burdens and pressure filled situations were stacking up and piling on top of me, I had a real choice to make. Quit and accept defeat or persevere and bounce back better than ever.

I was face to face with hundreds of thousands of dollars worth of obligations to pay off with no apparent strategy of doing it. Despite the severity of the situation, I still knew deep down inside I was going to come out on top one way or another. I refused to quit. I refused to lose. I refused to accept any other outcome than to be successful. I just needed the right door to open.

I had hit a ceiling that I was determined to find a way to break through. I'm not ashamed to say that I sincerely prayed and asked God to help me and show me what to do to get out of the hole and to get the results I believed I was destined for. It's amazing how sometimes in life the answer you "think" you need isn't the real answer you actually need. I thought I needed a large sum of money for my life to change in my business. Yes I did need a lot of money, but I needed something else even more that would prove to be the key to unlock the flow of resources I was looking for. What I needed the most was *wisdom* in my relationships. I was unconsciously and unintentionally allowing toxic relationships and partnerships in my business that were draining me of time, energy, and money. It was my own lack of wisdom in setting healthy boundaries in business that had opened the door to the disappointing results I was getting.

I thought I needed to only learn real estate to succeed but I was overlooking the importance of the quality of relationships in my business. I paid a high price for that lesson but once I got it, I got it! I took that insight and began making the necessary relationship changes and adjustments to start seeing real progress and results in my life and business. I share this part of my journey because you too may have to make some relationship adjustments to experience the results you want in your financial life. *Right relationships produce acceleration while wrong relationships produce deceleration!* Everyone won't be happy when you make these changes but we all must ask ourselves the question, *"Would I rather have the approval of others or would I rather have the results I want in life?"* In order to get the results we want in life, we must be willing to make tough decisions which will inevitably disappoint and anger others. If someone else gets angry at your progress and success, then that is proof they didn't need to be in your life in the first place. Your true relationships will always be happy for you when you succeed.

(This isn't a book on relationships but you won't be successful without having that understanding. Now back to real estate! ☺ *)*

The Deal That Changed It All

When I made the relationship changes I needed to make, my mind cleared up to begin to see new possibilities and new opportunities. I was on the hunt for something big. I just needed to see what it was. After several weeks of searching and digging for the right opportunity, I think I finally found it. I still was doing a couple small wholesale deals on single family houses to stay afloat and pay bills. *But I wasn't content to just "pay bills."* That's not why I got started in real estate. I got started in real estate to experience life changing results and I was determined to achieve it. I had heard "through the grapevine" of talking to other investors and older people that land development was where the big money was at in real estate. I didn't know the first thing about land development but I was already in a hole so I figured what do I have to lose? I was crazy enough to jump out of the boat of my comfort zone and take my shot. I still was hopeful and enthusiastic to get wealthy in real estate.

I called a real estate agent I knew and told her I was looking for a land development deal. She sent me a list of about 10 properties to look at. We drove around for a full day to go look at all the properties. I was inexperienced in this area but I trusted my intuition at this point. Out of all those properties there was only 1 that caught my attention and that had the possible potential to be the deal I was looking for.

I didn't know much about land flipping at the time but I had learned enough to know to send any potential land development deals to a civil engineer so they can evaluate the feasibility of the project. I sent a local engineer that property to look at. It had some environmental and aesthetic obstacles but it did indeed have potential to be something life changing based on the feedback of the engineer. I was probably getting on the engineer's nerves with all of the questions I was asking but I wanted to learn and know as much as I could so I could begin understanding the process. I learned the value of zoning, how to determine the density of units on a property, environmental pitfalls to watch for, how to communicate with city officials, and how to negotiate land deals with sellers and buyers. All of that on one deal! That was some real on the job training.

After 12 long months of going through the development and approval process, facing hurdle after hurdle, and getting the plans finalized, I experienced what I had read about and heard about from other real estate investors. Life-changing money! The property was a little over 23 acres and was eventually approved for 238 townhomes. Remember, on my first single family wholesale deal I made less than $1,000 after splitting it with a partner. However, on my first land flipping deal I made $1.3 million! I think I could get used to that ☺. I was indescribably happy, but more than that I was relieved that I could take care of my commitments and obligations as I like to keep my word to people and this allowed me to do that. So did I go to the beach and chill and drink lemonade? Heck no! If I could make this much on one deal, I wanted to see how I could do more and more of these deals. I was officially addicted to land flipping! I did enjoy it but I was more interested in duplicating it than stopping my progress by kicking back and relaxing.

Since that deal I have gone on to do countless other deals flipping over 1,000 residential lots, building new construction homes, acquiring commercial properties, and joint venturing with many others on deals. Land flipping was the niche I had been looking for. The more deals I did, the more I realized that there weren't many people who taught on this subject in a relevant and captivating way to make it easy to understand and applicable in the life of anyone. I am a firm believer that since we as humans all live on land we should at least understand the fundamentals of how land works and how we can make money with it. That's what this book and our content is all about at Mr. Flippy. Inspiring and educating everyday people to experience "wealth & riches with dirt & ditches." As you continue reading, we want you to be one of them!

CHAPTER 2

"THE SIMPLICITY OF LAND FLIPPING"

The Urgent Need For Land Flippers

In the United States, due to population growth and key driving economic factors, there is a chronic shortage of affordable housing units on the market today. The word "affordable" is very subjective and determined by the financial demographics of a particular market but a general description of affordable housing is your basic bread and butter housing, typically a 3 bed 2 bath or similar size house. Every major growth market in the country has national, regional, and local home builders that need new approved lots to build new houses to help supply this shortage. The majority of these builders do not want to go through the process and hurdles to locate and to get new sites approved to build on. This is where the big opportunity for people like you and me come in as a land flipper!

Even though most builders don't want to go through the land flipping process, they are more than happy to pay someone to bring them approved development projects so they can do what they do best – build. The reason these builders will pay such a high price for these approved sites is for one simple and old business cliché. "Time is money." Land flipping is a process that may take several months to complete, so if you bring a builder an approved development project it cuts months of time off of their process which allows them to start building so they can make money quicker. As a land flipper, we are providing a service to builders by locating, negotiating, entitling, and engineering a piece of land making it ready to be built upon. Instead of competing over pre-existing houses like wholesalers and house flippers, becoming a land flipper allows you operate in a low competition niche where you can create inventory vs. competing for existing inventory. As the old saying goes "niches produce riches." I am a living witness that the niche of land flipping is an arena that most people do not have the know-how or the mindset to navigate as it takes time and a specialized skill set to successfully complete a project. However, once you have mastered the art and science of land flipping, you literally can create limitless opportunities and paydays.

The Simple Steps To Flipping Land

When I was doing my very first land flipping deal, I honestly didn't have a clue what I was doing but I was pursuing the possibility of what I had heard from others. Instead of thinking of all the reasons it wouldn't work or why it was too good to be true, I had the willingness to take action to see for myself. I'm glad I didn't let fear hold me back because there really was a pot of gold at the end of the rainbow ☺. Even though I didn't know what I know today when I first got started, I did have enough sense to hire and surround myself with experts who could help me navigate the process. That is the same for you. You don't have to know everything to get started in land flipping. You just need to know who to connect to in order to be successful in this niche sector of real estate. I am sharing with you what I wish I would have known when I got started. There are several strategic relationships to build to be a successful land flipper:

* Real Estate Agents
* Wholesalers
* Civil Engineers
* Other Land Flippers

Real Estate Agents

Real Estate agents are vital in the land flipping process as they can have key connections to buyers, investors, and builders. As you start cultivating relationships in the world of real estate I would highly encourage you to start letting all the real estate agents you meet know that you are looking for land development projects in your market. I have personally done some of my best deals by working with strategic real estate agents in my area. Real estate agents can also be a great source of sending you potential land leads as they can search the MLS in your area or they can have the insight on off market properties as well. Obviously, every lead they send you won't necessarily be a deal but as you dig through the ones they send there is a high probability there will be a "diamond in the rough." As with any professional relationship all agents are not created equal. You may have to go through several contacts before connecting to the right ones. But it is well worth the process as the right real estate agent can connect you to both buyers & sellers to help you locate deals that you couldn't have found on your own.

Wholesalers

Wholesalers can be a great source of land development leads. As I mentioned in chapter 1, I initially got started in real estate as a wholesaler as that is the path of least resistance to start making some money in real estate. Wholesalers are typically trained to locate existing houses that have deferred maintenance and that need some range of renovation on them. This allows them to get a property under contract significantly below market value which creates a profit margin where they can simply "assign" their contract to an investor who wants to fix up the property. The wholesaler makes the difference between what they get the property under contract for with the seller and what the end buyer is willing to pay for it. Wholesalers very rarely have any knowledge of how to maximize a land deal as it is a specialized niche that must be cultivated and perfected. There are times when a house may have additional land with it or the existing zoning can be conducive to tear down the house and subdivide the lot into multiple building sites creating a greater profit margin. If you know how to effectively analyze a property as a land flipper, you can get some great deals through wholesalers.

Civil Engineers

Civil engineers are your secret weapon in navigating the complexities of land flipping. A qualified and effective civil engineer can literally make you millions of dollars in land flipping because they help to design the concept plan that you will use to sell your property to a buyer or investor. Civil engineers specialize in determining the maximum amount of units a piece of land can support. They also design the infrastructure of a development such as the roads, sewer, electric, and water lines. Just as an architect designs a building, a civil engineer designs the dirt that the building will go on.

Another valuable service a civil engineer provides is that they will actually do the presentations and public meetings when your plans go before local planning commissions and city officials to get your development concept approved. Civil engineers take a vacant piece of land in an undeveloped state and meticulously design the land to support buildings and structures in a way that will be aesthetically pleasing, functionally accessible, and financially profitable. That is why I said you don't have to know it all to be a land flipper. You just need to know the right people who can help you maximize your project in a feasible and profitable manner.

Other Land Flippers

Another valuable source of relationships to be successful as a land flipper is other land flippers. Experienced land flippers can be a great asset as they may have established buyer relationships with builders to help you move a property faster and possibly more profitably at times. Of course in this scenario they will want to be compensated which is fine if they are helping you to make significant money. In my own land flipping journey, I have partnered with many people on different deals to help maximize the profitability and feasibility of completing a land development project. As you begin letting your market know what you are looking for, you will cross paths with other land flippers and be able to establish key relationships to produce great results in your business. Our company "Mr. Flippy" also provides consulting and joint venture opportunities if you ever get a potential land lead in your area. If we can make the deal work, we will gladly split the profits with you and help you to make great money while learning the process (contact us at letsflip@mrflippy.com).

The Secret Number You Need To Know

Now that you know some of the key relationships you need to be a successful land flipper, now you need to know how to quickly evaluate a property on your handy dandy calculator. No matter what piece of land you look at there are two pieces of information you have to know to be able to quickly evaluate how many lots a property can get on it – Zoning & Property Size. Every established city has some type of zoning code for their local jurisdiction. Zoning determines the usage of a piece property and is vital in keeping a city's aesthetics and functionality up to modern day codes and standards. When it comes to land flipping, zoning is important because it defines the size and type of lots you can put on a piece of property. Once you develop the habit and consistency of evaluating land, it becomes second nature. We will look at a simple example of how evaluating a property using zoning and property size works.

In this example, the property is 1.5 acres and is zoned for 10,000 square foot residential lots. As a land flipper, you want to know how many lots you can get on this piece of land which will ultimately determine how much you can sell it for on the back end. The secret number to accurately evaluating the potential lot density on a piece of land is *43,560*. This number is the amount of total square feet in one acre of land. You will use this number on every single land deal as it is the universal standard of land size calculations. So in this example you would multiply 1.5 by 43,560 to give you the total amount of square feet of this property, which would be 65,340. Then you would take 65,340 and divide it by 10,000 which is the size lots the zoning allows in this example. 65,340 divided by 10,000 is 6.534. *(When calculating lot density you always round down to the lowest number since you can't have a partial lot)*. This leaves you with 6 lots. Now this is very simple math for quick analysis, but once you get deeper into the engineering and environmental study phase of land flipping it could affect the density some once you take into consideration any environmental limitations, roads, property setback lines, etc. If you know that you can get about 6 lots on this site, you can then take that number and multiply it by the amount that a builder/buyer would pay in your market for an approved lot. So say if a builder in your market would pay $20,000 per approved lot you could potentially sell this project for $120,000. Now it's simply a matter of getting the property at the right price from the seller. Knowing what you can sell the property for on the backend based on the amount of lots gives you a negotiating advantage because you know how high you can go on the purchase price and still make money.

To make sure you have a better understanding of this quick analysis process as a land flipper here is one more example to work through. In this example the land size is 4 acres, the zoning allows for 5,000 square foot lots, the seller is willing to sell the property for $180,000, and builders in this market are willing to pay $15,000 per approved lot (also called a "paper lot"). So here's how that math would work. Remember 43,560 is the universal secret number in evaluating land size on these deals. So in this example you would multiply 4 by 43,560 which gives you 174,240 total square feet on the property. The zoning allows for 5,000 square foot lots so you would divide 174,240 by 5,000 which gives you 34.848. Remember you always round down to the lowest number when calculating lot density so this would be 34 potential lots this property could have on it. In this example we said that builders are willing to pay $15,000 per approved lot. So now you would multiply $15,000 by 34 to give you $510,000. Finally you would subtract the sales price of $180,000 from $510,000 leaving you with $330,000. Just for hypothetical numbers let's say your expenses for engineering and miscellaneous fees were $50,000 in the process so you would subtract $50,000 from $330,000 leaving you with a profit of $280,000.

Does that sound like a good deal? I think so! This is not a fairy tale or "too good to be true" scenario. Land flipping can easily produce this level of results and greater. I have seen it over and over and over and I am still amazed at how lucrative and life changing land flipping is. Now you have the formula on how to quickly evaluate and analyze land flipping deals. So get out there and do some deals!

Due Diligence Checklist

As mentioned earlier in this chapter, your secret weapon on evaluating a piece of land is your civil engineer. They are licensed experts at evaluating the pitfalls and possibilities of a piece of vacant land. Even though you will need to hire a civil engineer in the process to get a land flipping deal completed, there are simple checklist items you can do to expedite the process and to gain a better knowledge of a piece of land to ensure it is a good fit to successfully sell to a buyer. Here are the checklist items you will need to check to make sure you can flip your land deal to a buyer:

1. Confirm general details of property *(lot size, location, purchase price, etc.)*
2. Confirm the current & potential zoning
3. Confirm sewer/septic availability
4. Confirm water/electricity availability
5. Calculate back end sales analysis based on the zoning, lot size, lot density, and buyer's price range to determine economic feasibility of the project *(use previous deal analysis examples as a reference in "The Secret Number You Need To Know" section)*

These are the real steps to apply on actual land flipping deals that can make you real money. The purpose of this book isn't to give you theories or just book knowledge. This book is designed to give you the actual steps and tools to begin evaluating, acquiring, and profitably exiting land flipping projects that can literally change your financial life. You now have the connections you need to cultivate, the formula to analyze the numbers, and the due diligence checklist needed to effectively navigate a land flipping deal.

Land Flipping Is Like Bottled Water

Yeah I know what you're thinking. How in the world is land flipping like bottled water? Here is a simple example that shows the exponential profit potential of land flipping using a 24 pack of bottled water as the example. Imagine when you go in a grocery store in the water and drink aisle. All grocery stores sell 24 packs of bottled water. They will slightly range in price depending on the branding and quality of the packaging but on average a 24 pack of water will be around $5 give or take. We will use $5 as the number for this example. So a whole case of 24 bottles of water is $5. However, you can walk closer to the register at the same grocery story and that same brand and size of bottled water will sell for $1-$2 for just one bottle. By breaking up the case and selling the bottles of water individually, you can make $24-$48 on the same $5 case of bottled water. This perfectly relates to how land flipping can work.

The $5 case of bottled water represents 5 acres of land. That 5 acres of land can sell for $50,000 as a whole. However, through the knowledge and application of zoning and subdividing a piece of land into smaller lots, you can get lets say 25 lots on that same 5 acres. So now instead of selling the 5 acres as one package, you can sell the land as individual lots for let's say $10,000 per lot. When you multiply 25 by $10,000 you get $250,000. So on the same exact amount of land you go from potentially selling it for $50,000 to being able to sell it for $250,000 which is $200,000 more just be breaking it up and selling it as lots instead of a whole parcel. This is the reality of how land flipping can produce exponential returns and life changing money. Land flipping isn't for some special class of people or business expert. I firmly believe since all of us walk on and live on land everyday *(unless you're an astronaut or a submarine operator)* that we should have at least a foundational understanding of how to maximize and benefit from the wealth producing potential of land. I hope this book is helping to expand your knowledge and awareness of you being able to do land flipping in your own life.

CHAPTER 3

"LAND FLIPPING SUCCESS HABITS"

The #1 Disease In Business

Just a few short years ago, the whole world was impacted by the covid pandemic. This pandemic shut down whole cities, businesses, and lifestyles for several months. Even though this impacted so many people across the world, in the world of business, personal dreams, and fulfilling our destiny, there is one disease that is far greater than covid. Analysis Paralysis!

I learned about this disease when I first got into real estate. Far too many people are infected by this disease. Analysis Paralysis is the chronic condition of gathering information without ever taking action on the information you learn. Of course we all must gain knowledge and insight before we can effectively take a course of action. However *"the acquisition of knowledge is useless without the application of knowledge."* I personally know people who have told me time and time again what goal and desire they have only to see them years later and they are still thinking about doing it. I want to use this last chapter to motivate and inspire you to not allow this crippling disease of Analysis Paralysis to hold you back from experiencing tremendous breakthrough and success not just as a land flipper but in your overall life.

The purpose of this book isn't to give you every single detail about land flipping and land development. The truth is that you don't need every single detail to succeed. You just need the fundamental understanding of what to do and who to connect to in order to start getting results. This book has laid out the real world process of how to shorten your learning curve to start getting real results in your own life as a land flipper. Some things you will never fully learn until you actually start doing it and gain experiential knowledge. Everything I have shared in this course is from actually doing deals not from theory.

The two main ingredients that fuel the disease of Analysis Paralysis are:
1. *The fear of failure*
2. *Waiting for perfect circumstances*

The only failure in life is failing to take action and failing to make necessary adjustments when something isn't working. You can't fail if you make up your mind you won't stop until you succeed. We all will experience disappointments and setbacks, but it's how we respond that will determine our ultimate success and outcome. Too many people wait for everything to be "perfect" to take action. The truth is that all circumstances may never be "perfect" to do something life changing. There will always be a reason to not do something or to put it off until a better time. The only problem is that a better time may never come. The best time to do something is when you are inspired to do it while it is fresh on your heart and mind because if you wait until everything is "perfect" the motivation and momentum to do it can subside. This puts you in danger of being a statistic of the *"shoulda woulda coulda"* crowd. Don't let that be you. Make up your mind that you will take massive action on the knowledge you have learned and that you won't stop until you experience the life changing results you are looking for. Go out there and make "wealth & riches with dirt & ditches!"

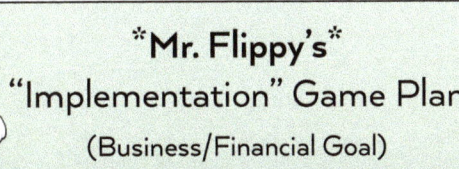

Mr. Flippy's "Implementation" Game Plan
(Business/Financial Goal)

QUESTIONS	ANSWERS
What is the #1 improvement you want to see in your finances/business?	
How will your life be better as a result of this change happening?	
What has held you back from seeing this change up to this point?	
In order to see this change happen, in what ways can "you" change?	
When do you want to see this change occur and what action steps will you take to see it through?	

Mr. Flippy's
SERVICES & PRODUCTS

* Live Land Flipping Events & Seminars
* #1 Land Flipping Digital Course
* Creative Land Flipping & Real Estate Music
* Joint Venture Opportunities On Actual Deals
* Custom Presentations & Speaking Services To Groups or Teams
* Deal Analysis & Consulting

For More Information Contact Us At:

www.mrflippy.com
letsflip@mrflippy.com

About the Author:

William Vaughn IV a.k.a "Mr. Flippy" is a dynamic and creative entrepreneur with a niche skillset of successfully navigating the various nuances of land development. He is an avid learner allowing him to continuously fine tune his mindset and knowledge base in this niche market empowering him to expand into more deals and opportunities to help others do the same. William has a great passion to inspire and teach others how to achieve "Wealth & Riches With Dirt & Ditches." He is happily married to his wife Amber, and is also the blessed father of his 3 children – Sariyah, William V, and Aliyah.

www.ingramcontent.com/pod-product-compliance
Ingram Content Group UK Ltd.
Pitfield, Milton Keynes, MK11 3LW, UK
UKHW022119230426
12048UKWH00010BA/605